BOX
INSPECTOR

and other important
JOBS FOR CATS

Swerling & Lazar

© 2017 Lisa Swerling & Ralph Lazar
Published by Last Lemon Productions
60 Woodside Dr. San Anselmo, CA 94960, USA

ISBN 978-0-9997316-0-4

First Printing, 2017

www.lastlemon.com

This book is
dedicated to

KIC

BELLA

&

CAPTAIN FLOOF

Table of Contents

IMPORTANT CAT JOBS

You humans are not quite sure what us cats do all day.

I tell you, there is a lot we do, a plethora of unspoken, critical jobs that go un-noticed. We're there, in the background, day in, day out, working, without complaint.

ICE CREAM
QUALITY ASSESSOR

LAP WARMER

ALARM CLOCK

MASSAGE
THERAPIST

MORALE BOOSTER

CHIEF PILLOW
APPRAISER

SLEEP STUDY
SPECIALIST

ASSISTANT SUITCASE PACKER

PAPER WEIGHT

CHIEF
TECHNOLOGY
OFFICER

LAUNDRY PRESS

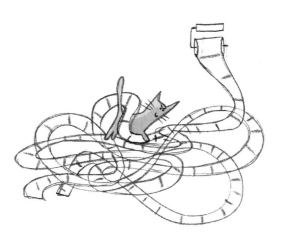

HEAD OF TOILET
PAPER OPERATIONS

STAIRCASE
SUPERVISOR

GIFTWRAP TECHNICIAN

LITERARY CRITIC

ASSISTANT BEDSHEET
CHANGER

PEST CONTROL

POLTERGEIST CHASER

STRESS
RELIEVER

CHIEF HOUSE PLANT DECOMMISSIONER

FOOD CRITIC

BOX INSPECTOR

BED SUPERVISOR

FOOD SURVEYOR

HEAD COZY

DOCUMENT EDITOR

BATH TESTER

LAUNDRY STANDARDS DIRECTOR

SHOPPING BAG CHECKER

GHOST SPOTTER

PEN PUSHER

BATHROOM ATTENDANT

GRAVITY
APPRAISER

CHIEF PROCRASTINATOR

WATER INSPECTOR

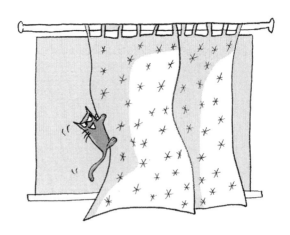

CURTAIN PATROL

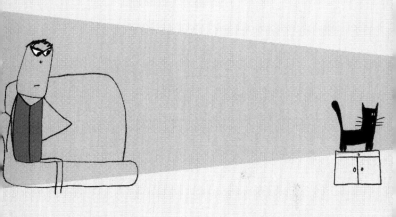

TV SUPERVISOR

NINJA

CHIEF SPIDER
SPOTTER

NIGHT WATCHMAN

SOUS CHEF

LIBRARIAN

BOX SHREDDER

UNDERWEAR AUDITOR

BAG CHECKER

WALL
INSPECTOR

SHOELACE
MONITOR

QUILT TESTER

33

KEYBOARD
WARMER

MAIL INSPECTOR

NEIGHBORHOOD
WATCH

INTERIOR
DESIGNER

DISHWASHING
ASSISTANT

SUNBEAM
ANALYST

GLOBAL HEAD OF
CUPBOARD INSPECTION

SECURITY OFFICER

PASSAGE CHAPERONE

ROAST CHICKEN
FOCUS GROUP

SNUGGLE AGENT

COMMANDER OF THE
101ST AIRBORNE
PIZZA REGIMENT

TRAILBLAZER

FENG SHUI
CONSULTANT

WILDLIFE
EXPERT

MATTRESS TESTER

HUNTER

BOSS

Although us cats can do just about everything better than humans, there are still some

USES FOR HUMANS

SOFA
WARMER

LADDER

WAITER

DOORMAN

VANTAGE
POINT

WHOLE BODY PILLOW

LANDING PAD

OBSTACLE
COURSE
TRAINER

FRIEND WITH
BENEFITS

THE QUESTIONS
CATS ASK

Who is feeding me?

How are you feeding me?
Which bowl are you using?
Why haven't you fed me yet?
When are you feeding me?
What are you feeding me?

What are you cooking?

What does this button do?

Why are you exactly 8 minutes later
than usual getting home from work?
No, seriously why? We almost starved
waiting for you!!

Do you love me
as much as
I love you?

59

What's in that bag?
And that bag?

What are you doing behind
that door?

will I fit in?

Where are you going?

Can I have some. Can I? Can I?
Pleaaaaase....

Can I sit with you while
you pee?

Can I go out? Can I go out? Can I go out? Can I go out?

So when is
the real food coming?

Snack? Snack?
Snack?

Why are you in my spot?

Your bed? No, this is
my bed. Actually, my room
and my house.

65

Shall we
have a staring
competition

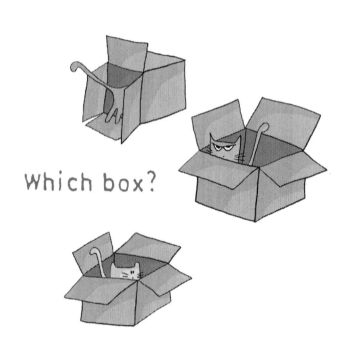

Which box?

Wanna play?

What's for dinner?

Would you move your
hand over a bit?

What else can
I teach you?

SIGNS THAT YOU'RE A CRAZY CAT PARENT

Are YOU a crazy cat parent?

No, of course you're not.
Or maybe you are.

If one or more of these apply
to you, then by definition,
you are.

You watch a show
specifically for your
cat's enjoyment,
not your own.

You apologize when it's
time to leave for work.

..and you ask how their day
was when you get home.

You REALLY need to pee
but you won't get up
because there's a cat
on your lap.

You get super-excited by home
deliveries because you know
your cat's about to get an
empty box to play in.

Cat gets
most of the bed.

You have framed photos
of your cats on your
desk at work.

You're secretly hoping someone
invents a way of messaging your
cat while you're at work, so you
can check in on it.

You spend more time in the supermarket's cat food aisle than all the other aisles combined.

If the sofa is occupied,
you're fine to take the
uncomfortable chair.

You refuse to stroke
other cats because it
feels like a betrayal.

You're sensitive to your cat's every mood

Angry	Annoyed	Happy	Tense	Welcoming
Sad	Contemplative	Coy	Bellicose	Enigmatic
Shy	Threatening	Bashful	Bitter	Calm

The food you feed your cat costs more than your own.

You have more photos of cats on your phone than humans.

You lie awake all night
because your cat is
sleeping on your stomach,
so you can't move.

Do you ever notice your cat behaving strangely?

Maybe something is going on?

IS YOUR CAT PERHAPS AN ALIEN?

DOES YOUR CAT SPEND
A LOT OF TIME JUST
WATCHING YOU?

DOES IT SUDDENLY DASH
ACROSS THE ROOM?

RUSHING TO PICK UP
A MESSAGE FROM
THE MOTHERSHIP
PERCHANCE?

DESPITE FEARING
WATER, DOES IT
CONSTANTLY
ANALYZE IT?

WHAT'S ALL THIS
STUFF WITH BOXES?
TRAINING FOR
TELEPORTING?

WHAT *IS* PURRING?
DO WE ACTUALLY KNOW?
COMMUNICATING WITH
THE MOTHERSHIP?

DOES IT STUDY
WHAT YOU EAT?

DOES IT MONITOR
EVERYTHING
YOU DO ONLINE?

DOES IT SEE THINGS
THAT YOU DON'T?

DOES IT SEEM VERY
INTERESTED IN
TASTING YOU?

YES, YOUR CAT
IS AN ALIEN.

OUR SECOND CAT BOOK:

"Be Hungry 24/7 and other secrets to being a cat"
is AVAILABLE FROM AMAZON now!

BE
HUNGRY
24/7

and other secrets to
BEING A CAT

Swerling & Lazar

HAPPINESS IS...
more than 1,000 illustrated happy moments

The A to Z of HAPPINESS

Lisa Swerling & Ralph Lazar

From the creators of the "Happiness is..."
online global phenomenon, comes a new book with over 1000
heartwarmingly happy-making illustrations.

The hundreds of happy moments include:
Finding money in an old pair of jeans...
Exchanging a friendly glance with a stranger...
The smell of the earth after rain...
Holding a small hand...
Scratching an itch...

This book reminds us of the hundreds of small happy
moments that happen every day - if only we take the
time to notice them.

Happiness is...

finding a power outlet
at the airport

finding something useful
on a bulletin board

chill time

when the hiccups stop

remembering the
whole dream from
the night before

spinning
on a chair

SMILE

You're on HAROLD'S PLANET

Swerling & Lazar

HAROLD'S
PLANET

A compendium of over three hundred and fifty funny, surreal and heartwarming cartoons. It's the first book in a new series showcasing the very best of Harold's Planet from the first twenty years.

GUIDE TO BASIC KNOTS

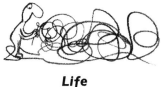

Reef   Bowline   Figure 8

Overhead   Half hitch   Slip

Life

Def: BYEBYEMISSAMERICANPIE
DROVEMYCHEVYTOTHE
LEVEEBUTTHELEVEEWASDRY
-OPHOBIA

The fear of getting an annoying song stuck in your head

"It is one of the blessings of old friends that you can afford to be stupid with them."

-Ralph Waldo Emerson

merlot merlittle

The joy of wine

Swerling & Lazar

A compendium of Harold's Planet wine-themed cartoons that are sure to bring a big smile to all wine-lovers - from those who enjoy a simple glass with a meal, to the most sophisticated of connoisseurs.

EXCERPTS FROM "MERLOT MERLITTLE THE JOY OF WINE"

an illustrated book by Lisa Swerling & Ralph Lazar
Available on Amazon

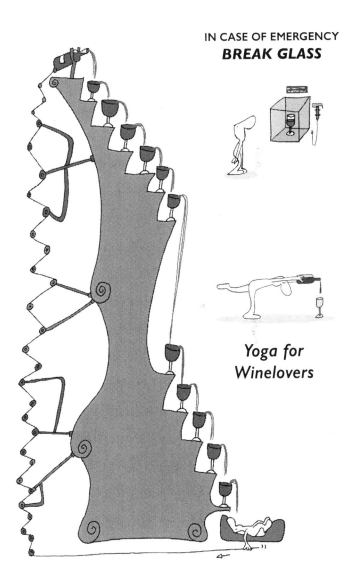

IN CASE OF EMERGENCY
BREAK GLASS

Yoga for Winelovers

BE AFRAID

then

do
it

anyway :)

Swerling & Lazar

101 Nuggets of Inspiration from **HAROLD'S PLANET**

A compendium of cartoons that will leave you feeling invigorated, refreshed, delighted, perhaps a little discombobulated and DEFINITELY inspired to DARE to do things your OWN way!

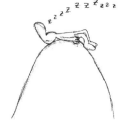

HOW TO AVOID
GETTING STRESSED
AT WORK

Don't go to work.

SPUTNIK + CLYDE

ARCHEE

JEN

TOMMIE

DREW

JULES

DORY

DOUGLA

ROCKEY

LOLA

GINGER

SIRIL

We also couldn't have made this book without the help of:

BELLA

FREY

EDNA

EDGAR

ANUBIS and BAAL

ERNIE

BOBA FETT

EEVEE

MONTY

SHEBA

LILLY

MOO

MAX

SOPHIE

OUNCE

ABOUT THE AUTHORS

Lisa Swerling & Ralph Lazar live in California.

They are the creators of the popular illustrated project Happiness Is..., which has sold nearly half a million books and has over three million followers online.

They also wrote and illustrated the New York Times bestseller Me Without You.

VISIT US ONLINE

We have a huge library of funny and sweet cat cartoons online at www.lastlemon.com/cats

And we have a quarter of a million followers on Facebook here www.facebook.com/itsthecatpage

Printed in Poland
by Amazon Fulfillment
Poland Sp. z o.o., Wrocław